Wants You To Be Debt Free

An inspirational guide to breaking the chains of debt and
empowering your life to be the faithful steward God wants
you to be.

Sam Peters

Prov. 3:6

Published by
Sampet Books
Wheelersburg, OH 45694

ISBN 978-0-6151-5363-6

If you need additional copies of this book and your local bookstore does not have it in stock you may purchase additional copies from **www.lulu.com** or by contacting Sam directly at **spete71@juno.com**.

This book is dedicated first to God for His inspiration to write something that would bless others and help them escape the pressure of financial problems.
Secondly, I'd like to thank my wife, Joyce for her encouragement while I stayed up late writing.
I'd also like to thank Allen and Dee Elrod for their mentoring and friendship over the past 15 years.
Thanks to Colleen for her help in finishing the book cover.

Contents

Foreword

Money only comes with one instruction - "In God We Trust" - and every payday we pray "Dear God I'm trusting you to make it last!"

Next to the subject of Love, money and possessions is the most covered topic in the Bible. Throughout the Old and New Testament, God gives us insight on finance, possessions, work ethic, saving, benevolence, etc. There are about 500 verses dealing with prayer, less than 500 verses on faith, but more than 2000 verses on money and possessions. Because the Bible deals with the subject so much, it should be a priority for Christians to understand something about it.

The purpose of this book is to teach sound Biblical principles for eliminating debt from your life, and help you establish the financial discipline to become the faithful stewards God wants you to be. It is my prayer that this book will bless you and lift the burden of debt from your heart.

Chapter One - Slaves to the Lender

Most people that struggle with debt and money woes tend to suffer in silence. In many homes, it is a private, embarrassing situation that too often continues as an ignored affliction. It begins as a blister, but later becomes a raging cancer, eating away at the quality of life God wants us to have.

It's difficult for most people to admit that they need help managing their financial affairs. A great majority of us would like to think of ourselves as reasonably intelligent adults, capable of making sound decisions. Unfortunately, when dealing with money, we've gotten most of our education through heredity. We've learned how to tie our shoes usually by age six. We learn how to drive a car by the time we're sixteen. By our twentieth birthday, most of us know how to earn a living. Yet, as grown adults, we still don't know how to manage our money. If you're like me, you learned most of what you know about finance by the successes or failures of your parents. We've never been taught the fundamentals of money management.

You may be, like many people I've met, under the notion that your situation is unique. Perhaps you think you are the only person with financial challenges. The good news/bad news is that you're not alone. Household debt levels are increasing at a staggering rate, exceeding income by more than 8%[1]. The average credit card holder has an average of $9200 of debt according to CardWeb.com.

Outward appearances can be deceiving. The families with big houses, new cars, new boats, etc., often have just as much trouble making ends meet as you.

The Bible shares some very instructional and empowering thoughts on the subject of finance and debt. One of my favorites comes from Proverbs:

> *Proverbs 22:7 - The rich rules over the poor, and the borrower becomes the lender's slave - NASB*

Do you ever feel like that verse is your life's verse? Do you feel like rich, prosperous people make all the rules? Does it feel like you are a slave to your debt? God wants to set you free from that bondage. God wants His people to have the right attitude about money and prosper as a witness to His goodness and blessing.

Before we can effectively pursue the eradication of debt from your life, we must establish a foundation to build on. I believe this foundation must be laid in the cement of Truth from God's Word. Our attitude about money, God's purpose for wealth and stewardship are the building blocks for any successful financial plan. If your attitude about wealth is confused or inappropriate, no plan in the world will remove the trouble money will bring to your heart. Understanding God's purpose for our prosperity helps us make sound decisions regarding our money.

Many Christians believe that "money is the root of all evil." This misquote of 1 Timothy 6:10 has led some to feel that God desires that we be poor and destitute. In fact, many wear their poverty as a medal of honor, when in truth, God would like them to be blessed and prosper. In the context of that chapter in 1 Timothy, Paul writes to young Timothy that there were those in the early church that wandered from the faith because they loved money more than God. He continues by saying that because of that, they were pierced through with many sorrows. Paul's desire is for Timothy to understand that earthly riches are temporary, and to exercise diligence in obtaining eternal riches. His warning deals with the attitude Timothy should have regarding wealth. If you're not wealthy, Paul says not to be consumed by it, but be content that you have food and clothing. God demands that He be our top priority. When we covet the wealth of the world more than the wealth of God, our priorities are wrong. This will in turn cause us to use poor judgment in our financial decisions.

I believe it's entirely possible that some people struggle with finances because God knows our heart and priorities about money aren't right. I believe that money makes a good person better, and a bad person worse. If your priorities are right, your decisions will be right as well. If you had the additional wealth, wouldn't you like to do more about the spreading of the Gospel and the support of the ministry? Are there people in need that you'd like to help? Wouldn't your example of stewardship be an inspiration to others and a wonderful testimony to the grace of God?

I've been blessed to know many Christian millionaires. They have shared with me the blessings they've received because they had it in their abilities to fund many Christian ministries and projects over the years. I know of one individual that donated $1 million to build a home for unwed mothers. I know of another that purchased equipment for a church that cost in the hundreds of thousands. I know of people that have fully paid college tuition for young people desiring to enter the ministry. The stories are endless of Godly people that are prosperous, but with the right attitude about wealth.

When you acknowledge that everything belongs to God, you realize that what wealth you gain is just an advance from God on the wealth he has in store for you later. (De. 8:16-18, Ps.24:1, Ps. 50:10, Hag. 2:8)

The Old Testament warns of the trouble that can come to a household in Proverbs 15:27 - *"He that is greedy of gain troubles his own house;"*. An improper attitude about money can cause a lot of tension among couples. More divorces are caused because of financial pressure than any other reason. In today's society of consumption and immediate gratification, husbands and wives indulge themselves with spending habits that are larger than their paycheck. I've talked with many couples that are quick to point at the other partner's spending habits as the source of problem in their marriage. Of course, their own spending habits are completely justified in their eyes. When we haphazardly spend we are indulging our own greed. We must keep our attitude in check when it comes to the temptation to spend impulsively. Let's call it what it is - greed. If we were to be honest, most impulse spending doesn't satisfy. Once the newness has worn off, we are left with buyer's remorse and the credit card bill to go with it.

The Bible has many references to greed, but there are none more poignant than the example of Judas. For thirty pieces of silver he betrayed Jesus (Mt. 26:15 & 16). The wrong attitude about money can cause hurt in the lives of so many.

So what is the right attitude to have about money? I really like the lesson taught by Jesus in the parable of the Talents - Mt. 25:14-30. This parable deals with stewardship. Though it is speaking of spiritual stewardship, the analogy is sound financial advice as well. Three servants were entrusted with money from a wealthy man leaving on a journey. Two of the servants traded with the money and earned more money. One of the servants was fearful and greedy. This servant hid the money in the ground. When the wealthy man returned from his journey he examined the three servants as to what they had accomplished with his money. The two that earned a profit were entrusted with even more. The third was punished because of his fear and laziness.

God has entrusted us with many things; our families, the work of the church, our jobs, our abilities, our wealth. He is like that wealthy man in the parable. He wants us to take what is already His, and wisely use it in a way that allows it to grow. If God has granted you the ability to earn an income, He desires to see you use it wisely. God wants you to be a good steward of your money. When we faithfully utilize what God has given us, He entrusts us with even more. When we squander what God has given, He takes it away.

Being a good steward of your money requires that you manage it as wisely as you can. By maintaining a proper attitude about money and wealth, you can do it.

Along the line of financial attitude, let me cover a common problem I see today. More and more couples are maintaining multiple checking and credit accounts in separate names. In the many years I've dealt with financial affairs, I've never seen this concept work very well, if at all. When you investigate the justification for having these separate accounts, you quite often come up with a totally different problem - a lack of trust. When you lack trust in a relationship, you usually end up with a broken relationship. The Bible talks about a man and a woman coming together as husband and wife and they become as one. In today's society, they become one only in shared sleeping arrangements. They've got mortgages in separate names, credit cards in separate names, checking accounts that are his, hers and ours. This lack of commitment to share in the marriage will most likely spell doom down the road. When I see this arrangement spring up later in a marriage, it's usually because one or both of them have poor financial habits. These habits have driven a wedge of mistrust between the two. You can regain that trust when you change the bad habits to good ones and begin to employ sound financial strategies. If you want your marriage to be a joint relationship - get joint accounts.

Too many families suffer quietly from the bondage of debt and poverty. God wants to set us free not only from sin, but any bondage that prevents us from being the joyous follower of Christ He intended us to be. There is no need for you to suffer with the pain, depression and worry brought on by your financial situation. You can make a change and you can make it now!

If you are enslaved by debt, begin your journey to freedom with this chapter's prayer:

> *Lord, help me to get free from the bondage of debt in my life. Help me to understand your desires for my financial affairs and to maintain a Godly attitude about money. As a child of the King, let my life be a prosperous witness to the glory of God. In Christ's name I pray, Amen.*

Chapter Two - Charge It!

The credit system has been around a very long time. In Exodus 22:25 & 26 it speaks of giving a pledge, or collateral as a means of securing a loan.

> *"If you lend money to one of my people among you who is needy, do not be like a moneylender; charge him no interest. If you take your neighbor's cloak as a pledge, return it to him by sunset" - NIV*

The modern credit system we know today began when Isaac Singer came up with a new way to peddle his sewing machines when most families were living a very meager existence. In 1856 he devised a plan whereby a family could buy his Singer sewing machine for $5 down and $5 a month. His sales picked up, and buying on credit was the reason why. In 1916, Arthur Morris expanded the concept of buying on credit, by creating the installment loan. Look where we are today. Who would have imagined that we would have gotten to the point where you can barely function in society without a credit card? If you go to purchase an appliance at Sears today, they don't want to talk about what it costs, they emphasize the minimum payment. You look at that new TV and you say to yourself, "I can afford $35 per month, I'll take it." You do the same thing with the sofa, the bedroom set, the washer, the chain saw, and so on. Pretty soon your minimum payments total hundreds of dollars each month. That's not all. Because we are making so many minimum payments, we get ourselves into a paycheck to paycheck situation. Because we are living paycheck to paycheck, we make only the minimum payment on those installment purchases. The result - many of the things we purchased are worn out or broken before we even pay it off!

To help you better understand how we got to where we are today, I'd like you to consider one of the unique phenomena of our century - the "Baby Boomer" era. In my opinion, this never before seen explosion of people has driven every aspect of today's world financial condition. When this boom began in the mid 1940's and throughout the Fifties and early Sixties, it literally has driven our economy and industry. The old saying goes, "Necessity is the mother of invention." This boom opened the door to invention. When you have this many people being born in such a short period of time, it's bound to create some necessity. In the fifties companies that catered to young married couples with babies grew large seemingly overnight. Baby food companies like Gerber became mainstays in the American home. As these babies grew into toddlers, companies like Fisher-Price, Mattel and Hasbro were there to take advantage of a need for toys. Can you remember your first Barbie or Tonka truck? As we entered the Seventies our toddlers were entering teen-hood. With that came a demand for clothing and entertainment. This drove the growth of companies like Levi Strauss and Wrangler. We also saw a clamoring to purchase records, and attend large concerts, etc. Our teens were into Rock n' Roll. The Saturday night jamboree was replaced with the Beatles at Shea Stadium. As a teen-ager in that era, most of us learned to spend our money for things we wanted right now. We grew up in a time of reasonable prosperity and learned to be a nation of instant gratification. With the technology of television, business realized quickly that they could entice us with advertising around the clock. "Buy now, pay later", was the ad-speak of the day. As we entered into early adult life we had become accustomed to having what we want, when we want. As we married and settled down we had to have our newly furnished homes with wall to wall carpeting and all the trimmings. We needed two new cars. We had to have new furniture as well.

One of the inventions that allowed all of this to happen was only about three inches long and two inches high. It was so thin you could slip it in a wallet. We were told "never leave home without it." That's right; it was the amazing credit card. The proliferation of credit cards in our society has made it too easy for the consumer to get into debt. The language of the card contract and how the interest is calculated and how the minimum payment is to be paid is so complicated that many of us are concerned with only one thing - "what's my minimum payment?" We don't want to know how the interest is calculated on the average daily periodic balance, or that the rate charged on cash advances is calculated differently than a purchase. Or that fees assessed on the card are charged as cash advances. "Just tell me what my minimum payment is" says the consumer. With that, we "charge" headlong into debt, if you'll pardon the pun.

We now live in the era of debt in this country. As the Boomers get closer to retirement they are becoming increasingly aware that they will have a poor quality of life during their golden years if they don't get out of debt and start saving money. That necessity has created another industry - the mortgage lending industry. It's always been there, but now the pie is so large, that many of the companies bombarding us with mailers and advertising weren't even around five or ten years ago. Industry and commerce understand the Boomers better than they understand themselves. Man in the masses is totally predictable. Business is taking advantage of a predictable situation.

Today, you can purchase your groceries on your credit card. Have you stopped to think how much that head of lettuce or gallon of milk cost you at 18% interest?! The cost of convenience is high when you're dealing with credit cards. If you have a $3,000 balance at 19.8% interest and pay the minimum payments, it will take you approximately 39 years to pay it off! You will pay over $10,000 in interest charges! And that assumes you make no new charges. Is it really worth the convenience?

> *Chapter prayer:*
> *Lord, I thank you for opening my eyes to*
> *the pitfalls of debt. Help me to eliminate*
> *debt from my life and determine in my*
> *heart to avoid these traps in the future.*
> *In Jesus' name I pray, Amen.*

Chapter Three - Know the Rules

When you were a kid, did you ever play a game with someone that kept changing the rules of the game, or wouldn't tell you all of the rules until it was convenient for them? You probably felt pretty upset by it. It's hard to win the game if you don't know the rules. In the credit game, the lenders know all of the rules, but would really prefer you didn't. In this chapter I'll share with you some of the rules of the game so that you can win.

Regardless of your knowledge of the rules, you can't just take your ball and go home. If you are under an obligation of debt, you need to pursue every means possible to meet that obligation. Psalms 37:21 states that *"The wicked borrows, and pays not again..."* It is not appropriate to borrow with the intention to default on your debt. God would have you make every effort to repay your debt.

As I mentioned before, the credit card companies and the lenders know that man in the masses is totally predictable. This predictability drives their advertising to the consumer. The incessant bombarding of ad's have practically brainwashed us to believe that if it's on TV, it has to be true. The result is that when we hear fancy pitches to get a credit card, we can't wait to sign up. Because we've accepted that status is everything, we just have to have that "Gold" credit card. When we feel the need to up our status even further, we apply for the "Platinum" card. What's next, the super, duper, double titanium card? How do these cards work? What does all of that fine print mean?

Credit cards have a lot of things going on that most of us don't understand. If you've ever looked at your monthly statement, it probably looks pretty complicated. Most of us only look at two things on a credit card statement, the **minimum payment** amount and the **due date**. There are a number of things that are critical for you to know if you are going to use a credit card.

One of the enticing gimmicks offered by the credit card industry is the super low interest rates available to you if you transfer your existing balances to their card. Here's an example of how it works for some people. You complete an application to transfer an existing balance of $6,000 from a high interest rate card to a new lower rate card. You receive your credit card in the mail and a letter stating that you have a $2,300 limit. Because all of the fine print is difficult to understand, you assume that either they transferred the balance and approved you for an additional amount, or that they transferred nothing and that you were just approved for a new card. Delirious with joy at the untold wealth in your hand, you immediately run out and charge $350 at the nearest department store. You run to the next store and try to charge more. However, your card is rejected. Why? You find out that you've exceeded your limit. How can that be? You had a $2,300 limit. You rush home and call the credit card company. They explain to you that your available amount was only $300. They had transferred a portion of the balance from the other card ($2,000), and left you with an available credit line of only

$300. The first purchase was approved because it was within an acceptable range of your limit. The charge was approved, but you were charged an over the limit fee as well. That fee was added to your balance. Not only was it added, but it begins to accrue interest immediately - there is no grace period on cash advances and fees assessed. The interest charged on the fee is at a much higher rate than purchases - typically 18% and up. Because you exceeded your limit, your low introductory rate was escalated as well. Instead of paying 9.9%, you're over 18% again. That kind of defeated the purpose of transferring the balance didn't it? By the way, when you get that first statement, don't be surprised to have a large payment due to get you below your limit again and cover the interest charges on the fees, etc. Before you say that this couldn't happen, let me assure you it did to a client of mine. To say they were shocked would be an understatement.

I know of another example where a person was near their limit and when the annual fee was applied to the account, it pushed them over by $16. This event wasn't even a charge! The over the limit fees pushed them even higher over the limit. The new interest rate for the card was 23.99%!

Credit card companies are in the business to make a profit. If you think you will out smart them by doing the interest rate shuffle, think again. They make up the rules, remember? In all of that fine print you signed, they have built in safeguards that prevent them from losing money. There are events that trigger an immediate rise in your interest rate. In addition to the above example, your rate might be increased if your payment is received even one day late. Your card might have a clause that allows the interest rate to go up if you make no new charges in the first 90 - 180 days. In some cases, introductory rates are for transferred balances only. New purchases and cash advances are at a higher rate.

For those of you that pay your new charges in full every month to avoid any interest charges, they've come up with a way to profit from you too. If you're one of those smarties that pay in full, they'll charge you a high annual fee, or increase the rate on the balance. Some card companies have shortened their grace period from 30 days to 20. Many times you're notified of these changes, but it's usually buried in the print and notices on your credit card statement.

Card companies can increase even your fixed interest rate without your approval with a 15 day notice. Often, this notice comes in your statement as additional mail. Most people tend to discard it as junk mail advertising from the company and never read it. One day you look at your statement and like magic, your interest rate has gone up. No wonder that card never gets paid off.

Other high jinx that occurs with credit cards is the computation of interest based on the daily periodic balance and the fluctuating billing cycle. Because the card companies change the number of days in their billing cycle, it affects the average daily balance of your account. The interest charged on an average daily balance can be higher than the real balance at the end of the month. The date that your previous payment was received and credited to your account affects this average balance too. If possible, get a card that charges interest on a monthly periodic rate.

The method used to calculate minimum payment varies among lending institutions, however, I've found that card companies typically charge you about 2% of the balance as a minimum payment or $15 whichever is greater. Since many people are over-extended with debt, they tend to make only the minimum payment. The card companies love it when you do that. Often the minimum payment barely covers the interest. The best approach to take is a fixed payment rather than a revolving payment plan. As an example, let's suppose you have a $5,000 credit balance and opt to repay it on the typical revolving debt schedule mentioned above. Your initial minimum payment would be $125 gradually decreasing to $15 per month. At 18%, it would take you 22 years and 9 months to repay that loan. If you were to pay it back at a fixed payment of $125 per month, you would eliminate that debt in 5 years, 2 months. Additionally, you would save $4,233 in interest with the fixed payment method. So when the advertisement tells you that their card pays you back, remember how pay backs worked when you were a kid. It still works the same way.

Does all this worry you? It should. Unfortunately, the society we live in today makes it virtually impossible to conduct business without a credit card. One avenue you may want to consider to help with this dilemma is obtaining a debit card. Debit cards are issued by most banking institutions that handle checking accounts. They work just like a check, but carry the convenience of the card. When you use it to make a purchase the amount is automatically deducted from your checking account. If possible get a debit card with a small limit ($500 - $1,000). In this way you can use it when you need to charge something and don't have the immediate cash, yet you are limited as to how much trouble you can get into. You should be aware that some businesses won't accept a debit card, or put large holds on your checking account while you're using their services, such as hotels and rental car companies. In those instances you may find it necessary to get a credit card with a small limit. Again, you can use it to reserve things like hotel rooms. When you check out and pay, use the debit card. This keeps your money liquid for use while you travel, but prevents you from extending your debt. I would also encourage you not to chase the "unbelievable deals" offered by credit card companies - frequent flier miles and bonus points toward buying a new car. These incentives just encourage you to charge even more. Find a card with a reasonably low interest rate and keep it paid off. It may cost you an annual fee to have a $0 balance account, but the necessity of having a card today may be worth it.

Chapter prayer:

God, You know all things. I've played a game without knowledge of the rules. Your Word teaches me that "The heart of the prudent gets knowledge; and the ear of the wise seeks knowledge." Help me to understand the things that are needful for my household to be free from the burden of debt. In Jesus' name I pray, Amen.

Chapter Four - Fail to Plan, Plan to Fail

There's a quote I've heard a number of times, "Most people don't plan to fail, they fail to plan." I don't know who to credit for those wise words, but they are certainly true. Forethought can prevent a world of woe brought on by poor financial decisions. In a successful diet and fitness plan you count the calories. In a successful financial fitness plan, you must count the cost. Count the cost of your decisions. Think about the total cost a decision will render. Without a plan, you have little or no control over your financial matters. Your money is controlling you, instead of you controlling your money. A little planning can help you avoid heartache and embarrassment later.

In His parables, Christ enjoins us to count the cost of following Him with a short financial illustration. In the Gospel of Luke, He states:

> *Luke 14:28-30 - For which of you, intending to build a tower, does not sit down first and count the cost, whether he has enough to finish it - Lest, after he has laid the foundation, and is not able to finish, all who see it begin to mock him, saying, "This man began to build and was not able to finish it." NKJ*

One of the first steps needed to remedy financial problems is to begin a budget. Before you can achieve your financial goals, you must first know where you are now. Most families do not have a thorough written budget. They have what I call a "sorta-kinda" budget. They "sorta-kinda" know what they spend their money on. Many couples with money problems use the ostrich approach to dealing with it - they stick their heads in the sand and pretend it doesn't exist. They will sit down with their spouse and discuss the bills - "WHEN IT'S A GOOD TIME." They know they have a lot of debt, but they're afraid to add it up. I know this can be a bit unnerving, but it is essential.

Budgeting need not be a stressful time. I encourage you to prayerfully begin this process by acknowledging God as your leader and encourager. Proverbs 3:6 says, *"In all thy ways acknowledge Him, and He shall direct thy paths."*

Creating a written budget begins with finding out what you have spent money on in the past. This will require a little work on your part. I suggest setting aside 2 - 4 hours on a Saturday afternoon. Turn off the TV. Send the kids to Grandma's. Put on some relaxing music. Then get the shoe box out of the closet and begin. If you don't keep your financial records in a shoe box, congratulations, you probably have a file system. If you are technologically advanced enough to keep your records on a computer, better yet - print out the past 12 months.

In a spiral ring notebook, place a budget category at the top of each page as needed for the things you spend money on. (I've included a sample category list and a budget page in the appendix). As you review your receipts and canceled checks, write the amount on the appropriate page. Go back 12 months for the best results. You may find that you spend a large amount of money in cash and have no record of what you've spent. If this is the case, you should minimize this practice immediately. A budget will only work if you can monitor what you spend. If you must spend cash, insist on getting a receipt. If you know you regularly spend cash on certain items, estimate how much you spend and write it in appropriately.

Additionally, you may find that there are occasional expenditures that happen each year but not monthly. For example, car repairs and home repairs may be something you spend money on each year. You should budget for those expenditures. You may spend a larger amount on clothing around Christmas, and just before school starts. Again, you should budget for those shopping trips.

After you've listed all of your expenditures, total them up and divide by 12, (or whatever time period you used). This is your current budget for each category. List this amount on a budget page and realistically discuss what areas seem to have excessive spending. If there are categories with excessive spending, mutually decide how much you can successfully trim from that category and then stick to it. Write out a new projected budget with the new amounts listed. You must conscientiously monitor your spending to determine that you are staying on the budget.

One of your goals with this budget should be to eliminate debt. I'll be discussing ways to accomplish that in another chapter. You should also look for ways to begin saving your money more effectively. Every family needs an emergency fund and should also invest for things like retirement (it'll be here someday), and education for their children. This budget is the starting spot.

Now that you've determined where the money goes, look at a few key areas and determine how much goes to certain categories. For instance, what is your debt to income ratio? If you are a married homeowner and more than 36% of your gross income goes to paying debt, you have a debt problem.

What is your tax burden? Do you get a large tax refund every year? If so, change your federal withholdings. If you get a federal tax refund of $2000 every year, that's the equivalent of giving $166 every month to the government interest free. Would $166 per month relieve some of your financial stress?

How much are you saving? You should strive to save at least 10% of your gross income every month. Are you tithing appropriately? Are you overpaying for basic things? Your results may astound you when you see them in black and white.

The next measuring stick to review is your net worth. Many think that net worth only applies to the wealthy. However, net worth is an important measuring stick of any sound financial plan. As your net worth increases, it provides you a barometer of how you're doing with your financial plan. If it isn't increasing, then you haven't made sound choices with your money. Determining your net worth is simple. Take your gross assets (cash, investments and estimated value of possessions - what you could sell everything for at an estate sale), and subtract your liabilities (what you owe other people). The difference is your net worth. The larger your net worth is, the better your quality of life.

Part of your planning process may require you to educate yourself and possibly get some professional financial help.

> *Proverbs 1:5 ...let the wise listen and add to their learning, and let the discerning get guidance- NIV*

Most of us are not schooled on the detailed aspects of how money works so we need to educate ourselves. Reading this book is a good start toward that end. In addition to that, you may find that the help of a financial professional is needed. A competent financial professional will take the time to understand your situation and advise you of the options available to you.

Be wary of celebrity guru's that give you a quick answer to your problem. While the information they dispense may be accurate information, they may not understand your situation well enough to advise you, or may give you only part of the information you need. If any financial professional isn't asking you lots of questions before they begin to provide you with solutions, run quickly! My attitude in working with families has been to ask enough questions that I can put myself in their position. Then I ask myself, if I was in their situation but knew what I know, what would I do?

There are a number of highly qualified professionals available to assist you in planning and obtaining financial freedom. Unfortunately, there are some that take advantage of you for a commission or don't care about you because you don't have much money to work with.

There is one company that lives by the motto, "We do what's right 100% of the time." My experience has been that they live up to that creed. That company is Primerica Financial Services (PFS), a subsidiary of the financial powerhouse, Citigroup. For more than 30 years this company has championed the cause of the middle and lower income family. Taking the time to know their client situations, they genuinely care about helping them realize financial independence. With over 100,000 representatives in North America and expanding globally, they are positioned to help ordinary families accomplish extraordinary things through a variety of financial solutions and services. Their representatives provide families with a complimentary Financial Needs Analysis (FNA) that gives them a snapshot of where they are and where they need to go to become debt free and financially independent. By providing this service for no fee, it provides an excellent environment for an open and honest conversation about your financial situation. If they are able to help you, you're better off than you were before, and if they are unable to help you, then you're no worse off and you received a free education and analysis of your situation.

One of the other aspects that I find refreshing about the representatives at PFS is that so many of them are attracted to the company because of the number of Christians that have chosen to give the Primerica opportunity a try. They are drawn to the high moral standards and ethics that the independent representatives demonstrate when they work with clients.

Not many of us were blessed with the financial savvy needed to evaluate our monetary situation. But ignorance of how money works is not an excuse to avoid working on our problem. Get help! Get it from a qualified person that is willing to take the time to know your situation and that cares enough about you to solve the problems. Those kinds of people have knowledge you don't have. They have resources you can't tap. And they will take the time that you never have to create a solution for your financial woes.

You now have a foundation to start on. You know where your money is going now. It's no longer a guessing game! Good stewardship can only happen in the fertile ground of knowledge. Reap the benefits!

> *Chapter prayer:*
> *Heavenly Father, as I begin to search out your solutions for my finances, I praise you for the relief I already feel from the knowledge that you are in control. With your help, I know I can overcome the bondage of debt. In Jesus' name I thank you, Amen.*

Chapter Five – Run the Race To Debt Freedom

We are told to run the Christian race with patience (Hebrews 12:1). The debt freedom race requires patience also. You probably didn't get into debt overnight, and it's almost a certainty you won't get out of debt overnight either. Debt freedom will take discipline. You will need to stick to your budget. You will have to avoid impulse spending and bad financial habits of the past. Finally, you will have to pay the debt.

One of the greatest ways to eliminate debt is to accelerate your payments. Even if you have no additional money to apply toward the debt, you can take what you are already paying and eliminate the debt much sooner with a little discipline to stick with it!

I've heard a lot of terms used to describe this process. My term is called "Stack and Roll." You "Stack" each of the debts together and determine how much your monthly fixed payment will be. Once you've decided on an amount, maintain that payment amount throughout the process. Don't get caught up in the minimum payment game the credit companies would like you to play.

The next step is to take the debt scheduled to pay off first and pay it off. If you've determined to accelerate your debt with an additional amount over and above the minimums, great! Take that extra amount and apply all of it to the debt scheduled to pay off first. (This may not be the debt with the highest interest rate). Once you've paid off this first debt, "Roll" this payment amount to the next lowest balance so that you are paying the regular payment and the amount you were paying for the other debt you paid off. Continue this with each debt until all debts are eliminated. Here is an example of how the system works:

Monthly Bills	Balance	Interest Rate	Current Pmt.	Projected Pay Off	Interest Pd.
Visa	$450	18.00%	$20	Mar-08	$103
Car	$5,500	12.00%	$191	Oct-08	$1,019
Student Loan	$2,741	10.00%	$50	Jan-12	$936
Student Loan	$3,779	10.00%	$50	Nov-15	$2,209
Mortgage	$32,768	8.00%	$328	Sep-19	$21,367
Total	**$45,238**		**$639**	**Sep-19**	**$25,635**

In this example, the current monthly amount paid toward debt is $639. The Debt Freedom date is September, 2019 with a total of $25,635 paid in interest alone. By doing a "Stack and Roll" on the existing debt and paying $639 every month until the total debt is paid off, look at what happens:

Monthly Bills	Mo. Pmt.	Accelerated Amt.	New Mo. Pmt.	Projected Pay Off	Interest saved
Visa	$20	$0	$20	Mar-08	$0
Car	$191	$20	$211	Sep-08	$4
Student Loan	$50	$211	$261	Apr-09	$244
Student Loan	$50	$261	$311	Nov-10	$929
Mortgage	$328	$311	$639	Feb-14	$6,783
Total	**$639**		**$639**	**Feb-14**	**$7,960**

Just by paying a fixed amount instead of the minimum payments the debt is paid off 67 months sooner. Additionally, there is a savings of $7,960 in interest payments! If you were to add an additional $50 every month to the payment plan and paid $689 every month, the debt would be eliminated by May 2013 and save a total of $9,903 in interest payments.

Many families already practice some sort of accelerated payment plan. If the minimum payment is $22, they send in $25. If it's $63, they send in $100. While this approach is better than paying just the minimums, there is a way to accelerate even faster with that little bit extra. Add up the little extra you typically send in on each debt, take the total amount and apply it to just the debt with the lowest balance. This will pay it off much faster and give you even more to accelerate with once it's paid off.

With the amount of debt hanging over the heads of the American consumer, the lending industry has begun circling above waiting for a victim to stumble and fall. Then they swoop down to feed on the carcass. If you are a homeowner you have probably been approached by some lender to consolidate your debt with a home equity loan. Do these loans make sense? How can you make sure it's the best solution for you? Let me try to clear up the confusion.

First, let me say that all lending institutions are regulated and have to meet very stringent rules and code of ethics. They are monitored to prevent discrimination and to ensure fair lending practices. My inference to circling buzzards has to do with how the institutions prey on the plight of the growing number of families that are struggling with debt. Their advertising tactics appear to be vulture-like in their intent. Having said that let me say that in some circumstances a debt consolidation loan makes sense for debt elimination. If you are considering borrowing against your home to eliminate debt, think of it this way – you don't need another loan, you need a solution! If the loan is a means to solve your debt problem, it will probably work for you. If it is a bandage to cover the bleeding, it probably won't work. At the root of your debt problem is an attitude about spending. Until you are ready to eliminate debt, you won't.

A home equity loan utilizes the equity built up in your home as collateral for a loan to pay off high interest, non-deductible debt. There are several cautions you should take when you consider a home equity loan, and I will discuss those later in this chapter. Home equity is easy to determine. The difference between what you owe on the home and the appraised value is the equity. This is the amount the lender could potentially lend you to pay off debt. If your house is worth $100,000 and the balance on the current mortgage is $70,000 you have $30,000 of equity. It is also expressed as a Loan to Value ratio – i.e. 70% LTV.

In theory, a home owner gets a home equity loan and pays off some or all of their credit card and high interest consumer debt. This often results in a much lower overall monthly payment. This savings allows the family to have more choices about money decisions.

Unfortunately, many of them choose to go right back into debt by charging their cards back up to the limit again, or by making new large purchases like cars and boats. This is a point of contention I have with most lending institutions. They know that the majority of consumers will work themselves back into debt and paycheck to paycheck situation again. I personally feel they have the opportunity and the responsibility to educate the consumer on how to get out of debt. Their negligence to do so highlights the fact that they don't want a consumer out of debt, they just want all of their debt moved under their roof. Some lenders even penalize you if you want to accelerate or pay off your debt early by charging additional fees and pre-payment penalties. Home equity loans can make a lot of sense if they can reduce your monthly payments and you are committed to using that savings to accelerate and eliminate debt.

There are a number of consolidation loans available: 1st mortgage, 2nd mortgage, Equity Lines of credit, balloon notes, adjustable rate mortgages, fixed mortgages, reverse mortgages, stepped payment loans, etc. It gets pretty confusing when you are looking for a solution. The two basic home equity loans are a first mortgage and a second mortgage.

A first mortgage home equity loan pays off your existing mortgages and some or all of your other consumer debts. As a first mortgage, the lender stands first in line should you default on your loan. The advantage of a first mortgage is that you will typically get more attractive options – lower rates, lower payments, and longer repayment terms. The interest paid on the loan probably qualifies as a tax deduction, but you should consult a tax professional on whether or not you qualify to take that deduction. The downside is that you may have a limited loan to value amount available and you may have to pay higher closing costs due to appraisal fees, title work, etc., related to first mortgages.

A second mortgage loan pays off any existing second and third mortgages along with some or all of your other debt. It stands second in line to recover debt in case of default. The advantage is that you can get short term loans with low closing costs without changing your first mortgage company that you may be pretty happy with. The interest paid on a second mortgage is usually tax deductible. Often, you will be able to borrow up to and possibly exceed the value of your home. The disadvantages are that the interest rates may be substantially higher and loans at or above the home value put you at high risk of default and losing your home. Should you decide to sell your home you could possibly owe more than you could sell it for.

You should look for a lender that does not require any up front or out of pocket costs. Insist on a lender that will give you a loan proposal without paying for it. If they give you a proposal without getting home value, income and credit information from you, be skeptical. They cannot give you a solid proposal without that information and you may find your final terms substantially different that the one you agreed to in the beginning. Be sure to get full disclosure of closing costs and monthly payment options prior to agreeing to a proposal. Appraisal fees, title document research, and discount fees are typical closing costs to review. They should be reasonable, and included in the final loan amount. You don't want to get to closing and find that you have to come up with several hundreds of dollars just to wrap it all up.

While I'm thinking about it, let's discuss interest rate. We have been brainwashed to think that interest rate is the most important determination of a loan decision. Interest paid is much more important that interest rate. Interest rate matters if you are going to take the full term to pay off the loan. What you should be asking is, "What does this loan cost me?" Interest rate is a percentage that is charged monthly against the unpaid balance. If you use the acceleration principles I'm teaching, you will have a much lower balance each month, thereby paying less money out of pocket toward interest. Many people falsely believe they can go down to their bank and get the 6 or 7% loan they saw advertised in the newspaper for a 90% LTV home equity loan. When they get a proposal for 10% they get offended as though the lender has a personal problem with them or their credit. Understand that when the lender loans against the maximum value of your home, they are at more risk than if they were only loaning at the 70% level. If you were to default they have to sell your home to recover the debt. There are a lot of factors that go into establishing an interest rate. Your credit history is just one factor. Other things like Loan to Value, job history, mortgage history, debt to income ratio, pride in ownership, etc., all play a role in determining your credit score and subsequent interest rate. Additionally, don't let the interest rate be such a determining factor if you're trying to solve a problem. Does the proposal solve the problem at hand – paycheck to paycheck, high interest, extended debt freedom date, etc.? If it does, don't let the interest rate be a major hang-up for you. Think of it this way, in your current paycheck to paycheck situation, what good does your 7% first mortgage do you? You have no extra money to accelerate, you won't be out of debt for many years, and you will pay back a large amount of interest.

When you receive a proposal you may be told that you have a certain interest rate, when in fact you have a higher rate. Most lenders quote the note rate to a customer. The note rate is the interest rate charged against the principal amount only and does not have all of the costs associated with the payment factored in. The Annual Percentage Rate, or APR takes into account the total costs paid by the homeowner. The APR can be 1 or 2 percent higher than the note rate. Ask your lender which rate they are quoting when you compare proposals.

How many years should you finance your loan for? A lot of consumer educators have taught that you should always take the shortest loan term affordable to cut down on the interest paid. I agree with this in principle but remind you that the purpose of a home equity loan is to solve a debt problem. With that in mind, do the homework on which term solves the problem the best. For example: If a 30 year loan frees up $400 a month verses $250 with a 15 year loan, and your problem was meeting monthly expenses, a 30 year loan may solve the problem best. I have had instances where a 30 year loan accelerated, paid off in 15 years 6 months. The 15 year loan didn't free up enough money to accelerate at all. It was more important to the family to have the choices available with the 30 year loan, than to remain on a very tight budget and a 15 year mortgage.

You should also ask the lender if they accept accelerated payments such as; bi-weekly or bi-monthly. Also, do they apply an accelerated payment immediately, or do they hold it until the end of the month. By holding it, they can charge you more daily interest on your balance. A bi-weekly payment essentially pays one extra payment every year. On a typical 30 year mortgage by-weekly payments will reduce the term of the mortgage by 9-11 years! More importantly, it saves you thousands of dollars!

Using the same example earlier in this chapter, let's see what a home equity loan might mean to a family.

Current Debt Schedule

Monthly Bills	Balance	Interest Rate	Current Pmt.	Projected Pay Off	Interest Pd.
Visa	$450	18.00%	$20	Mar-08	$103
Car	$5,500	12.00%	$191	Oct-08	$1,019
Student Loan	$2,741	10.00%	$50	Jan-12	$936
Student Loan	$3,779	10.00%	$50	Nov-15	$2,209
Mortgage	$32,768	8.00%	$328	Sep-19	$21,367
Total	$45,238		$639	Sep-19	$25,635

A new 30 year first mortgage of $47,000 would payoff all of the above debt including closing costs of the loan. The new monthly payment would be $395/mo. on a 9.5% loan. This frees up $244 every month for the borrower. By paying half of the payment ever 14 days ($197.50 bi-weekly), the homeowner pays an extra payment per year. They need to take $33 per month of the savings to make the extra payment. If they were to then to add another $77 per month to the principal due ($100/mo. total), they pay off the loan in September 2019. The same time they would pay it off without a loan. The benefit is that this still leaves them with $134 every month to meet everyday living expenses. If they were to invest that amount in a mutual fund averaging 10% annually, they could potentially accumulate $47,549 by the time the mortgage was paid off! Now this family is debt free and has an extra $47,000 saved! All of this accomplished with the same money they spend every month now.

Actual loan rates, terms and fund performance of

course vary with each individual. The numbers used are for illustration purposes only. Individuals should consult their financial professionals for specifics before pursuing any financial solution.

I would also remind you to exercise caution when using a home equity loan to consolidate debt. While it may solve your debt dilemma, you are putting your home at risk. Should circumstances arise that prevent you from making your house payment, you could lose it in foreclosure. Your hard earned equity is a valuable resource, be sure you can meet your new obligations down the road.

Chapter prayer:
Heavenly Father, grant me the discipline to follow Your leading in eliminating debt from my life. As Your steward, I want to be found worthy of Your blessings. Thank You for bringing solutions to light that will help me. In the name of Jesus I ask it and claim it as done, Amen.

Chapter Six – Spending Habits

In Luke Chapter 15, we find the story of the Prodigal Son. This man took his inheritance and impulsively, squandered it on riotous living. As the text spells out, he had lots of friends while he had money, but as soon as the money was gone, so were his friends. Like the Prodigal Son, many people squander their money on impulsive pleasures without really counting the cost. The Prodigal's cost was great, he ended up broke and destitute, living off the slop fed to the pigs.

> Proverbs 21:20 "Stupid people spend their money as fast as they get it." – GNB

> Ecclesiastes 5:11 "The more you have, the more you spend, right up to the limits of your income." – Living Bible

Now that you are on your way to debt freedom, how can you prevent yourself from backsliding into compulsive spending again? First and foremost make it a matter of prayer everyday. This will help you to develop the habits necessary to have a sound financial game plan.

I've heard it said that if you are going to break a bad habit, you need a good one to replace it with. Develop good spending habits. Learn to value shop. My wife is a pro at it. She scours the newspaper and internet for sales, freebies and discounts. The result is that we are able to stay on budget and still have lots of fun and a high quality of life.

One of the key contributors to poor spending habits is a wasteful attitude. Often we purchase something on an impulse only to scratch our head later trying to remember what possessed us to buy it. Maybe it was the color. Maybe it was the appearance and feel. Maybe it was smart advertising. You see a great looking silver sports car in a commercial, winding its way along an open highway on a beautiful day. Instantly you project yourself sitting on the rich Corinthian leather driver's seat with the top down, designer sunglasses sitting halfway down the bridge of your nose as the wind blows through your perfectly styled hair. As you shift the car through every one of its gears, everyone seems to look at you as if they are saying, - "Who is that totally cool guy in the car?" The reality is you probably need a mini-van that seats seven! It's amazing how we can purchase something so totally unnecessary and inadequate. What a waste. The prophet Isaiah asks us, *"Why do you spend money on that which doesn't satisfy?" (Is. 55:2)*.

Do we always have to have the latest and greatest? Is it worth it to keep up with the neighbor next door? I find that most impulse spenders are also the greatest wasters. They waste their time, their resources and they waste their money. Learn to manage your schedule better. Have you heard the expression – "Time is money?" It really is. How many gallons of gas have you burned because you didn't plan the trip to the grocer while you were driving by it? How many hours have you spent running in circles because you didn't have a written plan? Have you ever thrown something out, only to discover later that you could have recycled it or used it somewhere else? When you purchase things that can be bought at a lower cost somewhere else, is that a wise use of your hard earned money? As Ben Franklin was quoted, "A penny saved, is a penny earned." How about the times you purchased an expensive gift for someone, when something handmade would have had more significance to them? In our house, when we give a gift to one another it has to be used, handmade, or something you don't need anymore.

You probably think we're really cheap skates, but we have come to enjoy the challenge of giving to others and putting careful thought into how it can show them they matter to us. It's easy to go to the department store and pick up some bottle of perfume, aftershave, or tie. It takes more effort to be creative and thoughtful. Let me give you an example. Every February my wife gets Valentine's Month. I give her something every day for the whole month. This year was leap year so I had to work really hard. I spent a total of $23 for the whole month. My wife couldn't wait to get home to see what surprise was in store for her that day. One day she got a gumball ring with a note in it asking her to be my steady – cost: 25 cents and some imagination. Her smile: priceless. She wore that ring to work the next day. Another gift was a fortune cookie from a local Chinese restaurant with a custom message from me. The restaurant manager thought my idea was so neat that they didn't even charge me for the fortune cookies, (they gave me a whole bag full). Every day she received some small gift that let her know I was thinking about her. I was the envy of everyone at her office. By the way for February 29th, I gave her a windup kangaroo with a note that said "I'm leaping with love for you." Yeah, I know it sounds corny, but she thought it was cute. That kangaroo still adorns our bathroom sink and reminds her everyday that I love her. I was able to make a real impact on her month for less than I would have spent for a dozen roses that would have lasted only a few days.

Another spending habit to get rid of – carrying and paying cash without getting a receipt. Money just burns a whole in some people's pocket. They have an overwhelming urge to spend it on things they normally can live without. I recommend not carrying any more cash in your pocket that is really necessary. As I'm writing this, I have total of $10 in my pocket, which is about $5 more than I usually carry. The reason there's so much is because I didn't spend my $5 from last week. I take lunch to the office nearly every day. We eat in more than we eat out.

My experience has been that when you spend cash and don't keep a receipt of your purchase, you tend to spend much more than you've planned in your budget. This eventually catches up to you when legitimate living expenses come due. This method of buying with cash may make it easy to hide purchases from your spouse, but it is one of the worst financial habits you can have.

When I was a teenager I would ask my mother for money all the time. She'd reach into a secret hiding place in her purse and pull out money for me. She said it was her "mad money" that my father didn't know about. While this may have been a unique approach to high finance for my mother, it wasn't the best habit for the family budget. Learn to track what you spend. You may learn a lot about how you manage your money.

Before you spend your hard earned income on a particular thing, ask yourself, "Do I really need this right now?" Ecclesiastes 6:9 says, *"Enjoy what you have rather than desiring what you don't have…" – NLT*

In Hebrews 13:5 we read that we are to, *"…be content with what you have…" – NIV*

If it's something that you do need, is it budgeted for? Will some other need in your life be put on the back burner because of this purchase? Will it make it difficult to pay your bills this month if you make this purchase? Think before you spend. Take a night to sleep on it if it's a big ticket item.

Developing good spending habits is one way you can demonstrate Godly stewardship in your life. One of the many ways our Provider meets our needs is by providing us with an income. He trusts us to be wise stewards of our money. When we spend impulsively and foolishly we are behaving as an untrustworthy servant. I firmly believe God grants and withholds financial blessing from us based on our ability to be wise with our money. I have a dear friend that gets by on a very meager existence. He does so because he makes every dollar count. I've witnessed the fact that he seems to get by better than others I know that make many times over what he does. I wonder if it is because his Heavenly Father knows what he has need of and provides it to him because of his faithful stewardship. How do your spending habits look?

When you throw your money around as though it grows on trees, there will be plenty of people around to help you spend it. When the money is gone and you are in need, where does your help come from? Learn from the Prodigal Son – develop good spending habits.

Chapter prayer:
Lord, when there have been times that I
have been thoughtless about my spending,
forgive me. I know it isn't a proper attitude
to have toward stewardship. Grant to me
wisdom and will power to develop better
spending habits. In Jesus gracious name I
ask it., Amen.

Chapter Seven – Establish an Emergency Fund

If you lost your job right now, how long would it be before you could not meet your monthly living expenses? Unfortunately, for most people that is two paychecks. Have you taken the time to think about that scenario? I've talked to too many homeless families that aren't victims of addiction or poor morals. They are victims to poor planning. When one or both of the wage earners lose an income, it doesn't take long to lose your possessions including your home.

Experience tells me that most of us don't plan for financial emergencies to happen. Yet, they happen to all of us. It may not be catastrophic, but nevertheless, even small financial emergencies can set us back. This is especially true when you are living paycheck to paycheck. There just isn't enough money to cover the inevitable and unexpected financial emergency. This situation causes many people to use their credit card for emergency purposes. In fact, I've had many people tell me during a financial interview that they only have a credit card for emergencies. Upon further investigation I usually find that a new dress was an emergency as was the vacation and the new drill press at the hardware store. Credit cards make lousy emergency funds. There is too much temptation to use it for other things that you haven't budgeted for. Before long you've maxed out your card and you can barely make the minimum payments. You may have lots of "stuff", but when the real emergency comes how will you deal with it? Look at an example of someone that didn't plan for a real emergency:

Luke 12:16-20
16 And he spake a parable unto them,
saying, The ground of a certain rich man
brought forth plentifully:

17 And he thought within himself, saying, What shall I do, because I have no room where to bestow my fruits?
18 And he said, This will I do: I will pull down my barns, and build greater; and there will I bestow all my fruits and my goods.
19 And I will say to my soul, Soul, thou hast much goods laid up for many years; take thine ease, eat, drink, and be merry.
20 But God said unto him, Thou fool, this night thy soul shall be required of thee: then whose shall those things be, which thou hast provided? - KJV

While I understand that the passage in Luke has a much deeper and eternal message for us to garner, it must be noticed that this man had no thought for tomorrow. Likewise, when we have no thought for a financial emergency, we are destined to suffer hardship.

There's a lesson to be learned about putting something away for a rainy day. Follow the analogy written by Solomon:

Proverbs 6:6-11 - You lazy fool, look at an ant. Watch it closely; let it teach you a thing or two.
Nobody has to tell it what to do. All summer it stores up food; at harvest it stockpiles provisions.
So how long are you going to laze around doing nothing? How long before you get out of bed?
A nap here, a nap there, a day off here, a day off there, sit back, take it easy—do you know what comes next?
Just this: You can look forward to a dirt-

*poor life, poverty your permanent
houseguest! – The Message*

Solomon shared his savings wisdom again in
Proverbs 21:20:

*"The wise man saves for the future, but the
foolish man spends whatever he gets" –
Living Bible*

For being such a wealthy nation, we have failed
miserably at saving any of that wealth. We are a nation of
consumers. The average family saves less than 5% of their
disposable income.

Establishing an emergency fund is one of the wisest
and one of the most prudent things you can do when
establishing a sound financial plan. I typically recommend
three months of income as a minimum goal. By setting
aside a little each payday you can quickly accumulate that
amount. The investment vehicles I usually recommend are
conservative investments that are readily accessible, but
more than an arms length away to prevent the temptation to
spend on things that are not really an emergency. Money
market accounts and municipal bond mutual funds are
conservative and provide you with competitive rates of
return. While savings accounts provide you with the
security of a guarantee, I feel they make poor emergency
fund vehicles. The rates of return on them are low and
after you factor in taxes and inflation may even give you a
negative net return. Additionally, they are too accessible
for some people. They can simply go to any ATM and
withdraw the money for any purpose at all. Remember,
this is ear marked for "emergencies". Emergencies are
those things that are not budgeted for, but absolutely
imperative – unexpected auto and home repairs, loss of
income, family hardship, etc.

I'm also not a huge fan of using Certificate of Deposits as an emergency fund. While CD's give you higher guarantees than passbook savings and they keep the money more than an arms length away to minimize impulse spending, you are penalized for early withdrawal of that money and that may make your rate of return less advantageous.

Everyone's situation is different. Your objectives, habits and disciplines may be met with any number of options. The key is to set that money aside systematically so that you will be prepared when the inevitable emergency arises.

The old axiom that a chain is as strong as its weakest link holds true with your financial plan as well. The best plan is only as strong as the weakest link. If you are doing everything right, but don't have an emergency fund established, the plan will fail as soon as an emergency happens. Don't overlook this much needed piece of your financial game plan. Begin setting money aside right now to cover emergencies.

Chapter prayer:
Father, I trust You when You said that You would always take care of us. I also believe I have a responsibility to be a faithful steward of what you provide for me. Grant me the discipline to save for a rainy day. With that emergency cushion I will have peace regarding any financial emergency that comes my way. Amen.

Chapter Eight – Tithing

One aspect of a sound financial plan that you won't hear much about from the secular experts, is the discipline of tithing. You will however hear it from me. From personal experience I've found that the more faithful I am in my giving, the more God seems to provide. I know that because of what He promised.

> *Malachi 3:10 - Bring the whole tithe into the storehouse, that there may be food in my house. Test me in this," says the LORD Almighty, "and see if I will not throw open the floodgates of heaven and pour out so much blessing that you will not have room enough for it.*

> *Proverbs 3:9-10 - Honor God with everything you own; give him the first and the best. Your barns will burst, your wine vats will brim over. – The Message*

Tithing puts a biblical perspective on money and wealth. We cannot commit to tithing without first putting our attitude on track with how God wants us to think about money.

I read that Martin Luther once said, "When a person is converted three conversions are necessary - Head, Heart, and Purse."

I think sometimes the purse conversion is the hardest. This stems from an overall attitude that our possessions belong to us. If that were true, then when you die, why don't you take it with you?

Our material possessions are on loan to us. Jehovah-Jireh (God our Provider) gives to us that we may be stewards of those gifts for His glory. Our motivation for giving should be because we are thankful to God for what He has done for us, and out of a Godly love. It is said that you can give without loving, but you cannot love without giving.

In the Old Testament God said that the tithe belonged to Him (Leviticus 27:30). If we gave or sold that tithe to someone else, then we were to add a 20 percent penalty to what we gave to the Temple. How would our giving be affected if we knew we would be penalized for not giving?

The New Testament teachings on giving do not establish a percentage for the giver. Paul provides guidance for us in 2 Corinthians chapter 9:

> *6Remember this: Whoever sows sparingly will also reap sparingly, and whoever sows generously will also reap generously. 7Each man should give what he has decided in his heart to give, not reluctantly or under compulsion, for God loves a cheerful giver. 8And God is able to make all grace abound to you, so that in all things at all times, having all that you need, you will abound in every good work.*

When it comes to giving we are to give freely, cheerfully, generously, and regularly. As part of your overall financial planning, you should prayerfully consider and commit to what God lays on your heart to give. We are not to give reluctantly or under compulsion – God loves a cheerful giver.

Christian giving asks us to look at our God given provisions and then, as God directs us through prayer and leading by His Spirit, set aside a percentage of those provisions as part of our worship, gratitude and desire for others to know this wonderful God.

Our poor financial attitude all too often influences our giving attitude. When you are overextended by debt and poor spending habits it is difficult to see your way clear to give regularly and cheerfully to God. The problem stems from a root issue of first giving "yourself" to God. Look at a passage again from 2 Corinthians chapter 8:

> *3For I testify that they gave as much as they were able, and even beyond their ability. Entirely on their own, 4they urgently pleaded with us for the privilege of sharing in this service to the saints. 5And they did not do as we expected, but they gave themselves first to the Lord and then to us in keeping with God's will.*

Paul is enthusiastically praising the church in Macedonia for their sacrificial giving. They gave beyond their ability because they first gave themselves to the Lord. I think many people find it easier to trust God with spiritual matters rather than their material matters. It is an act of faith to trust God in giving when the budget says there is no money to do so.

We are instructed to give to God the first fruits. That means we pay Him before we pay ourselves and before we pay anyone else. GULP! "That's hard to do!"

It is unless we do it on faith, trusting an all sufficient Lord to make it all work. Re-read the promises in Malachi 3 and Proverbs 3 at the beginning of this chapter. Do you believe God's promises?

Matthew 6:33 says: *"But seek first his kingdom and his righteousness, and all these things will be given to you as well."* If you are worried about how you will make ends meet if you begin tithing, Jesus said, I'll meet your needs if you put me first! It's a Lordship issue. Is God first in all areas of your life?

If your current financial situation is stressed and you are concerned about how you'll make ends meet if you begin to faithfully tithe, then start small. Purpose in your heart to begin giving, and then trust God to provide your needs. As God begins to meet your needs, stretch your faith by increasing what you give. The key is to involve God in the process – what would He have you give?

I am not necessarily a trumpet blower of prosperity preaching – that God wants everyone to be rich, though I do believe God wants to bless us for our faithfulness. I'd rather proclaim the law of sowing and reaping. As I mentioned earlier from Paul's writing to the Corinthian's, whoever sows sparingly will also reap sparingly, and whoever sows generously will also reap generously. God has given us many promises regarding our giving and promised blessing. In Proverbs 22:9 we read:

> *A generous man will himself be blessed, for*
> *he shares his food with the poor.*

Luke 6:38 contains this promise:

> *"Give, and it will be given to you. A good*
> *measure, pressed down, shaken together and*
> *running over, will be poured into your lap.*
> *For with the measure you use, it will be*
> *measured to you."*

Again in Proverbs, we read:
> *11:24 One man gives freely, yet gains even*
> *more; another withholds unduly, but comes*
> *to poverty. 25 A generous man will prosper;*
> *he who refreshes others will himself be*
> *refreshed.*

There are so many more promises God gives to those that are faithful to Him. God does desire to bless us. First, we must be faithful and obedient to Him in our giving.

I'm sometimes asked if a person should give 10% of their net or gross income. I would again encourage you to seek God's desire for your situation, but personally I lean on what Christ said:

> *Mt. 22:21 "Give to Caesar what is Caesar's, and to God what is God's."*

We are to give God what rightfully belongs to Him – a tithe of the first fruits (before taxes).

For some of you reading this, giving comes easy to you. God has given you the gift of generosity, (Romans 12:8). If you are such a person, you truly are a blessing to many. Undoubtedly, you have experienced God's promises because of your humble faithfulness. Continue to give generously, but be careful about your giving. Remain humble. Christ instructed us to avoid seeking acknowledgment for our giving by men. If we truly want to be rewarded by our Father in heaven, we are to give humbly, not letting our left hand know what our right hand is doing, (Mt. 6:1-3).

Tithing, like all of our financial commitments, is an important piece of our financial picture. Our attitude regarding it frames our overall commitment to Christ. He is either Lord of all, or not Lord at all. Do not overlook the importance of Christian giving as you begin to put your financial life back together. It may be the single most important factor in regaining financial health.

Chapter prayer:

Lord, for my unfaithfulness in giving, please forgive me. Help me to put you first in all of my decisions. Tithing as You would have me do is new territory for me. Guide me so that I might honor You with my first fruits and experience Your blessing and wonderful provision for my life. Amen.

Chapter Nine – Investing

Financial freedom is a personal definition. It isn't about how much money you've accumulated or how many possessions you own. Your definition of financial freedom would most likely be entirely different from mine if we were to put a dollar amount on it. Financial freedom must be couched in the setting of having choices. When you are able to make choices without regard to the financial impact to you or your family, you have freedom.

Once you have a handle on your debt situation and you've created and begun to work within a budget, you are well on your way to financial freedom. In order to have that freedom long-term, you need to set aside money for your long-term needs. In an earlier chapter I discussed establishing an emergency fund. Now I'd like to encourage you to set money aside for long-term goals and dreams.

Most people would like to retire someday. The sad fact is that according to a survey compiled by the Employee Benefit Research Institute, four out of every 10 people aged 55 or older; have less than $100,000 saved toward retirement. This is in light of the fact that most people will need 10 to 20 times more than that in order to have enough money to last their expected life time.

Workers with 401(k) plans have a significant advantage in saving for retirement, yet many do not maximize their options. One fourth of eligible employees do not participate in the plans they have. Only 10% contribute the maximum amount allowed. Of those employees that have employer matching funds of their investment, nearly half of them fail to maximize the matching contribution.

One of the biggest mistakes made with employer sponsored plans is the tragic wound employees inflict on themselves when they change employment. Nearly half of them take their hard earned savings as a lump-sum distribution rather than roll it over into an IRA to avoid taxes and penalties for early withdrawal.[2]

Some workers have convinced themselves that they will be "OK" in their retiring years, when in fact the statistics show that many are nowhere near their needed savings goals. According to the annual Retirement Confidence Survey, conducted by the nonprofit Employee Benefit Research Institute, more than 60 percent of workers are counting on receiving some income from traditional pension plans, when only 40 percent of workers are currently covered by them. In addition, many employers are eliminating pension plans from their benefit packages.

The National Retirement Risk Index, developed by the Center for Retirement Research at Boston College, shows that 45 percent of working-age households are "at risk" of failing to maintain their pre-retirement standard of living in retirement.

For workers without an employer sponsored plan and small business owners, there are retirement savings options available as well. Nearly every household is eligible to contribute to an Individual Retirement Account, yet only about 40% of households own one. Couple that with the fact that of those 40%, only about 26% made a contribution to their IRA according to an Investment Company Institute report in 2005[3]

The truth is that we have become a nation of consumers and have forgotten how to save. "Buy Now, Pay Later" takes on a whole new meaning when we think about it in light of retirement. Overindulgences at the sake of our long-term needs cannot be pleasing to God. Refer back to the verses mentioned in the chapter regarding Emergency Funds:

> *Proverbs 6:6-11 - You lazy fool, look at an*
> *ant. Watch it closely; let it teach you a thing*
> *or two.*

Nobody has to tell it what to do. All summer it stores up food; at harvest it stockpiles provisions.
So how long are you going to laze around doing nothing? How long before you get out of bed?
A nap here, a nap there, a day off here, a day off there, sit back, take it easy—do you know what comes next?
Just this: You can look forward to a dirt-poor life, poverty your permanent houseguest! – The Message

Proverbs 21:20: "The wise man saves for the future, but the foolish man spends whatever he gets" – Living Bible

What does all this say to those of us who believe God would have us be wise stewards of our finances? It says that we need to be consistently active and aware in and of our long-term savings.

I had a client and fellow brother in the Lord tell me once that he was trusting God to make things work out. While God will protect his faithful, we demonstrate a Godly arrogance when we fail to act wisely regarding God's present provision for our families. 1 Timothy 5:8 warns, *"If anyone does not provide for his relatives, and especially for his immediate family, he has denied the faith and is worse than an unbeliever."*

If we have it in our abilities to save for the future, it is prudent that we obediently do it. I like the wisdom from Proverbs 13:11:

Dishonest money dwindles away, but he who gathers money little by little makes it grow.

Little by little you can make an incredible difference to the quality of life you live in your golden years. Time and discipline are your friends when it comes to investing for the future.

The three most important words in investing are; "Objective, Objective, Objective". What do you want your money to do? If it is for your retirement, then there are many factors that determine that objective. If it is a college fund for your children, again, many factors come into play in determining the objective. Once you've clearly defined the objective of your investment, the key is matching the investment vehicle(s) to the objective.

There are several likely candidates for the investor looking to retire someday. Let me take a little time to explain them to you and how they might help you meet your retirement income goals.

First, consider taking part in your employer sponsored plan. These plans are, in most cases, a great way for you to invest on a pre-tax basis and often gain some employer matching contribution in the process. These plans may be a 401(k) plans in the case of larger companies, 403(b)(7) plans offered by non-profit employers such as churches, hospitals and schools, or they may be a Simplified Employee Pension Plan (SEP), or a Simple IRA used typically by small business.

The amount of money you can put aside each year in an employer sponsored plan varies depending on the plan your company has, but typically they allow you to put away more than you could in an Individual Retirement Account (IRA), by itself. For instance, in 2006 an employee could potentially contribute up to $15,000 per year in their 401(k) plan, $20,000 if they are over 50 and take advantage of the government allowed catch-up provision. The total amount of contribution including any employer matching funds is 25% of employee compensation or $44,000 whichever is less (2006 rules).

If you work for a non-profit company the maximum contribution is $15,000 with a $3000 catch-up provision for workers over 50.

The benefits to the employee, especially when the employer matches some percentage of their contributions can be substantial. A 30 year old worker earning $40,000/yr and contributing 6% per year with a 3% match and getting a 3% raise each year would have over $800,000 in their retirement account if they averaged 10% rate of return on their investment.

For those of you who feel that you can't afford to save for retirement, you can't afford not to save for retirement! Money, time and interest rate are the three factors that make you financially independent. Compound interest on your savings pays back more dividends than you think. There is a simple rule for approximating the effect of compound interest. It's called the Rule of 72. Simply put, you divide the number 72 by the interest rate you get on your money. The result is how many years it will take a lump sum of money to double. For instance; if you're getting 3% interest on your money, you divide 72 by 3 and you get 24. In other words you money will double every 24 years. Six percent interest doubles every 12 years and twelve percent interest doubles every 6 years. What does that mean for you? Look at this:

Number of Years	3%	6%	12%
0	$10,000	$10,000	$10,000
6			$20,000
12		$20,000	$40,000
18			$80,000
24	$20,000	$40,000	$160,000
30			$320,000
36		$80,000	$640,000

Another way to invest in your retirement is to contribute money to an IRA. There are two types available to you today – the Traditional IRA and the Roth IRA. Both are similar in many respects and differ in some very important respects. They are similar in that you can contribute 100% of your earned income up to $4000 per year with a $1000 additional catch-up contribution for workers over 50. Contributions made to your IRA are made on an after-tax basis; that is they are made from your net income. Both plans generally require you to wait until age 59 ½ to make withdrawals without penalty. There are exceptions to making withdrawals and you should consult a financial professional or a tax professional on your specific situation. Both plans grow on a tax-deferred basis.

The plans differ in that the Traditional plan may be tax deductible. If you are eligible to deduct your IRA contributions it lessens your taxable income and thereby reduces your tax. Your Traditional IRA is taxable only at withdrawal. As well, Traditional IRA's have a Required Minimum Distribution requirement at age 70 ½. The IRS requires that you begin taking a calculated minimum distribution of your retirement funds at that age. The withdrawals are then taxable.

The Roth IRA is not tax deductible. The trade-off is that provided you have had the Roth IRA for at least 5 years and are over age 59 ½ it can be withdrawn tax-free and penalty free. This can be a great benefit to the person who has maintained a Roth IRA for a number of years. The accumulation of funds built up in the investment is now accessible to the investor without tax and without penalty! A favorite saying of mine is, "It's not how much money you save, but how much you keep that counts."

The Roth IRA does not have the 70 ½ rule either. This can be a benefit to the worker that decides to work after that age or for some other reason does not need to access their money. It can continue to work for you as hard as you worked for it.

My description of the investment options covered is by no means exhaustive. Space does not permit me to go into all the detail needed to properly advise you on your particular situation, nor is this book intended to advise you on your specific situation. As I've mentioned before, I suggest you consult a qualified financial professional that can properly advise you on the retirement options that best suit your situation, objectives and time horizons.

If I could give you one piece of advice regarding investing for the future it is this – begin! The future will be here before you know it. He who gathers money little by little makes it grow.

Chapter prayer:
Lord, I have no idea what tomorrow holds.
In fact, you have told me not to worry
about what tomorrow holds because you
care for me. Help me not to worry about
my future by being faithful in putting a
little away for it. May you find me diligent
in things now and things tomorrow. Amen.

Benediction

What could you do for God if you achieved financial freedom? What could you do for your family if you were debt free? Your life has purpose! You were put on this earth to live a life pleasing to God. You are here to give Him glory. Does your checkbook honor God? Unfortunately, too many of us are embarrassed by our example of stewardship. I don't believe it is because we lack the desire to be faithful to God, I believe it is because we lack the education. The traditional money institutions have not demonstrated that they really care about families like yours. They are quick to issue us credit, but slow to teach us to be wise with it.

The Bible tells us in James 4:17 – *"Anyone, then, who knows the good he ought to do and doesn't do it, sins."*

God winked at our ignorance at one time, but now commands us to repent. When we didn't know any better perhaps we had an excuse for our financial mistakes. Now dear brother and sister in Christ – you know better.

My prayer is that this book has helped illuminate a path to freedom for you. I also pray that you will do me a favor – if this book has helped you, give God the praise. For it was this specific time that by His grace He chose to provide you with direction. Go forward in that grace and empowered to be the faithful steward He's always wanted you to be. Amen.

Appendix – Budget Planning

Income	Current	Projected
Employment Income		
Pension/Retirement		
Other Income		
Total Income		
Living Expenses		
Housing		
Rent		
Telephone		
Utilities		
Maintenance		
Furnishings		
Improvements		
Hired Help		
Other		
.		
Family		
Grocery/Dining Out		
Clothing		
Out of pocket medical		
Laundry/Dry Cleaning		
Child Care		
Out of pocket educational		
Legal		
Other (child support, etc)		
Transportation		
Gas & Oil		
Maintenance/Repair		
Travel		

Giving		
Charitable		
Non-charitable		
Leisure		
Vacation		
Hobbies		
Entertainment		
(movies, cable, etc.)		
Other		
Total Living Expenses		
Debt		
Mortgage Princ. & Int.		
Other Debt payments		
Total Debt Payments		
Insurance		
Individual Life		
Employee paid group life		
Health/Dental		
Homeowners		
Auto		
Private Mort. Insurance (PMI)		
Disability		
Other		
Total Insurance Premiums		

Savings		
Emergency Fund		
Retirement		
Education		
Goals & Dreams		
Total Savings		
Taxes		
Income		
Property		
Total Taxes		
Budget Summary		
Total Income		
Minus Total Expenses		
Shortfall/Surplus		

About the Author

Sam Peters has worked helping families understand and develop sound financial solutions since 1993. He has served in a variety of ministry capacities since 1982 and is currently the pastor of Minford United Methodist Church in Southern Ohio.

He has provided Bible-based financial seminars and sermons at numerous churches and is available to speak by appointment to churches and civic groups about God's instruction regarding wealth and finances. To get more information on scheduling a financial seminar for your church or group you may write to Sam at **spete71@juno.com**.

Notes

[1] Newsweek, August 8, 2006

[2] Statistics compiled from the 2004 Retirement Confidence Survey, Employee Benefit Research Institute; and **"Coming Up Short: The Challenge of 401(k) Plans,"** Alicia Munnell and Annika Sunden

[3] Investment Company Institute (ICI), Feb. 14, 2005